JOHN LEGEND
Get Lifted

CONTENTS

Piano/Vocal arrangements by John Nicholas

Cherry Lane Music Company
Director of Publications/Project Editor: Mark Phillips

ISBN 978-1-57560-823-5

Visit our website at www.cherrylane.com

John Legend

Whether you call it "fate" or "destiny" or "a calling," the fact is that some people are born to sing and create music. If you ask any of the "legends" in the music business, chances are you'll get a variation on the idea that music is and always has been the artist's most natural expression. The industry's latest "legend"—John Legend, actually—reveals that from the age of five or six, "I expected to be 'discovered.' I used to watch Michael Jackson on television and I figured I could do what he was doing." Music has been the central theme in the life of John Legend (born John Stephens) for as long as he can remember and now, some 20-odd years later, this multi-talented singer, songwriter, musician, arranger, and producer is fulfilling his childhood dreams and ambitions.

With *Get Lifted*, his major label debut album on Columbia Records, Legend demonstrates a rare ability to fuse the "feel" and vibe of classic old school soul music with the edgy flavor of 21st century hip-hop. While the romantic themes of traditional R&B permeate John's *Get Lifted*, there's also a street-worthy hipness and confidence: the sensuality of Marvin Gaye and the sincerity of Stevie Wonder merging with the directness of Snoop Dogg and the wit of Kanye West. Yet, John Legend is very much his own artist, gifted with singular talents and a unique sensibility.

Take "Ordinary People," one of the last tracks John worked on in the summer of 2004 for the album, which is executive-produced by hitmaker Kanye West (who also co-wrote and produced several tracks on the record). Recorded with John's simple and plaintive piano accompaniment, the song is, according to its creator, "...real, a composite of experiences. It's about love, not as a fantasy or fairytale, but as it really goes down between two people."

"Used to Love U," the infectious first single—co-written and produced by Kanye West—has, according to John, "...a bangin' hip-hop beat with a little Latin flavor and a soulful melody and vocal arrangement; it's a cool mix and fusion of different musical influences. We had the Black Eyed Peas' horns and guitar player on the track so you get a little of their flavor too."

With production by West, longtime musical associates Dave Tozer and Devo Harris, and Will.I.Am of the Black Eyed Peas, *Get Lifted* runs the gamut from the celebratory "Live It Up"—which John describes as "a personal testimony about how hard work and paying dues really does pay off"—to the thought-provoking "Refuge (When It's Cold Outside)," a spiritual, evocative ballad reminiscent of Lauryn Hill.

Among the impressive credits John's amassed in the last few years (which includes session work with Alicia Keys, Janet Jackson, Talib Kweli, Jay-Z, Britney Spears, Eve, Common, the Black Eyed Peas, and, of course, Kanye West), John is particularly proud of his work on "Everything Is Everything," a key cut on Hill's multi-platinum Grammy-winning *The Miseducation of Lauryn Hill*. "Through a friend of hers," says Legend, "I went to the studio when Lauryn was working on that record and I sang a couple of original songs for her and ended up playing piano on that song. I'm still very proud that that was the first major record I was on.

Counting Lauryn Hill, Stevie Wonder, Aretha Franklin, Curtis Mayfield, Al Green, and the O'Jays among his primary influences (along with a slew of gospel artists like Edwin Hawkins, Shirley

Caesar, Commissioned, John P. Kee, and James Cleveland he heard during his formative years), John Legend has combined his inspirations into a stunning new sound all his own. You can hear it on tracks like "She Don't Have to Know" and "Number One" (which features Kanye West), a pair of songs dealing with the age-old topic of infidelity. Of the latter, John says with a smile, "I guess you could say that's a 'guy' song. It's a bit tongue-in-cheek, basically saying, 'Hey, I know I cheated, but I'm a guy so what do you expect?' A lot of traditional R&B doesn't have that wit and swagger that you find in hip-hop, and that's what I wanted to include in my music."

On the sexier side, there's "Let's Get Lifted," a jaunty jeep-flavored cut and the sizzling "So High." In contrast, John also references his move from Springfield, Ohio, to attend school in Philadelphia through "Johnny's Gotta Go" (produced by Dave Tozer) and his love for family with the soulful "It Don't Have to Change (The Family Song)," which John says includes "…almost my entire family singing with me—my mom, my dad, my granny, my aunts and uncles and my siblings (two brothers and a sister). They're all on that track which has a doo-wop type of harmony arrangement."

Family roots are important to John and he recalls growing up in a distinctly musical household: "There was a piano in the house and I learned to play and read music early on. By the time I was eight or nine, I was playing in the local church for the choir. My grandma taught me a lot of the gospel songs and between lessons in classical music and singing and playing in church, I really developed my ear. I always loved the feeling when people responded to my singing and playing so I was already making little gospel records in high school. I was ambitious and just loved being onstage."

While his early exposure was to gospel, John was tuning into the radio by the time he was in his early teens listening to the likes of Jodeci, Boyz II Men, LL Cool J, and MC Hammer. With his obvious musical aptitude, Legend applied to various colleges for a scholarship and chose to go to the University of Pennsylvania, majoring in English. But between his studies and day jobs to keep money coming in, he spent practically every waking hour making music, recording CDs with his collegiate a cappella group, performing solo at talent shows and open mics, and directing the choir at a local church. Just months before starting work on *Get Lifted*, Legend finally ended a nine-year tenure as music and choir director at Bethel A.M.E. Church just outside Philly.

Being in Philadelphia in the late '90s allowed John exposure to some of the new artists—like Jill Scott and the Roots—who were at the nucleus of the burgeoning "neo-soul" movement. Committed to his craft, Legend continued performing in and around Philly and by 2000 he had expanded his audience base by doing shows in New York, Boston, Atlanta, and Washington, D.C. John frequently appeared on the same bill as such national R&B artists as Musiq, Jaheim, Amel Larrieux, Glenn Lewis, and Floetry when they were performing in the region and he began recording some of his live performances. Early CDs, such as 2000's *John Stephens*, and 2001's *Live at Jimmy's Uptown* generated sales at John's shows and on his website. Studio recordings—often done with college friend Dave Tozer—were made ". . . with the intent of getting a record deal. I never really got frustrated because there were always little 'victories'; plus, the real people, the audiences, liked me. You have to have a lot of stamina to keep going."

John's patience paid off: through his college roommate and collaborator Devo Harris, he met Kanye West (Harris's cousin), who was emerging as a hit-making producer for such acts as Jay-Z and Scarface and as an artist in his own right (via the now bestselling album *The College Dropout*). "I first met Kanye after he came to see one of my shows," Legend recalls. "It took awhile for us to start working together. The first time was when he had me come in to sing hooks on a couple of the songs that eventually made the *College Dropout* album. Then he gave me some beats to write to for my demo. After about an hour and a half of writing, I came back with a song called 'Do What I

Gotta Do,' based on a beat that sampled Aretha's 'Until You Come Back to Me.' He played that first song for a bunch of people and they all loved it, so we started working together more and more."

By late 2002, John had begun working with Kanye more often, playing piano, singing and co-writing two tracks on the *College Dropout* album while adding impressive credits to his ever-expanding resume: In 2003 John lent his vocal talent to "You Don't Know My Name," the lead single from the multi-platinum *The Diary of Alicia Keys* set, as well as co-writing, singing, and playing on the Kanye West remix of "If I Ain't Got You" from the same album. John's collaborations with West also include singing and playing piano on "Encore" and "Lucifer," tracks from Jay-Z's *The Black Album*. John was also lead singer and co-writer of "The Boogie That Be," from the Black Eyed Peas' *Elephunk* album.

With word-of-mouth spreading among industry execs and artists, John found himself making a number of guest appearances on different projects recorded in 2003 and out in 2004: He played keyboards on "Overnight Celebrity" (from Twista's *Kamikaze* CD); sang, played, and appeared in the video from Dilated Peoples' "This Way"; co-wrote and played on Janet Jackson's "I Want You"; co-wrote, played, and sang on "I Try," the lead single featuring Mary J. Blige, from Talib Kweli's *Beautiful Struggle* album (which also features John's work as lead vocalist and pianist on the track "Around My Way"). In addition to singing lead on Slum Village's "Selfish," John also played on sessions for Eve, Common, and Britney Spears while still performing at clubs and making two more independently produced live CDs—*Solo Sessions, Vol. 1: Live at the Knitting Factory* and *Live at SOB's*.

By late 2003 Kanye West had signed the multi-faceted Legend as the first artist to his production company, KonMan Entertainment, and a deal with Columbia Records soon followed. After signing with the label, Legend began the task of sorting through the many songs he'd written over the years, finally narrowing it down to 40 tunes—"in varying stages of development"—and working with West on the dozen or so songs that would make up the album. "I know that this album will set the tone for what happens with my recording career," John predicts. "The first song, 'Used to Love U,' is what the record-buying public will attach to me. It could become what I am known for."

Asked to describe his style, John says, "It's very soulful, rooted in gospel but with hip-hop beats and unique, witty lyrics, more 'major' than 'minor,' more of a 'feel good,' upbeat sound." That's exemplified by the aforementioned "Do What I Gotta Do" (featuring Kanye West), with its instantly memorable hook, and tunes like "I Can Change" (featuring Snoop Dogg), which John describes as "...my pimp redemption song! Like, I know I'm gonna get it right with this girl; I'm gonna repent. It's hip-hop with a gospel flavor and we have a choir singing on the track." Emulating the likes of "the gentle genius" Curtis Mayfield, John offers the beautifully tender "Stay with You," another fine example of his ability to bring his own well-crafted artistry to music that harks back to another day and time.

"I originally was given the name John Legend by a friend from Chicago because he thought I sounded like an old school artist," John confesses. "At first, I thought it was funny to be called 'Legend,' but then a lot of my friends started calling me that and it really caught on so much that more people were calling me 'Legend' than my real name. So I started to consider using it as my stage name. I knew it sounded a little presumptuous, but I figured it would definitely make me stand out from the pack. I figured it would make people pay attention to me. And once I have their attention, I hope to make them fall in love with my music. By being 'John Legend,' I put some pressure on myself and I'm gonna try to live up to it and I hope my music will live up to it."

One listen to the soulful yet edgy *Get Lifted* and there's no question that John Legend indeed delivers the real deal, living up to his name and beginning the next chapter in a career filled with promise and possibility.

Prelude

Words and Music by
John Stephens

go   with   me.   There's some - thing

new   for you   to   see.   Just re -

lax,   just re - lax.

Let's Get Lifted

Words and Music by
John Stephens, Kanye West
and Rick Shobin

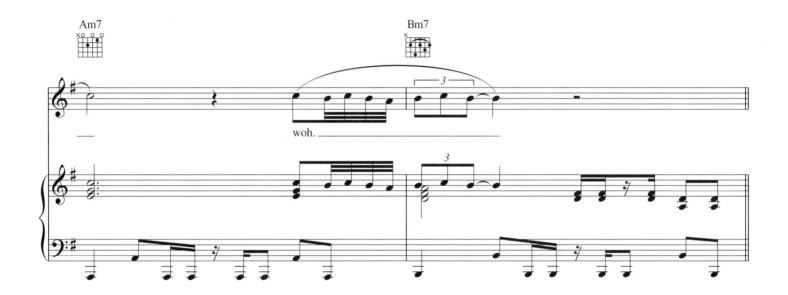

Used to Love U

Words and Music by
John Stephens and Kanye West

16

love __ you.
I ___ don't   love __ you.   Oh, I used __ to   love __ you.
Oh, _____

I _____ loved you. _____   And you gon-na miss me   now, _____
I ___ don't   love _ you.)

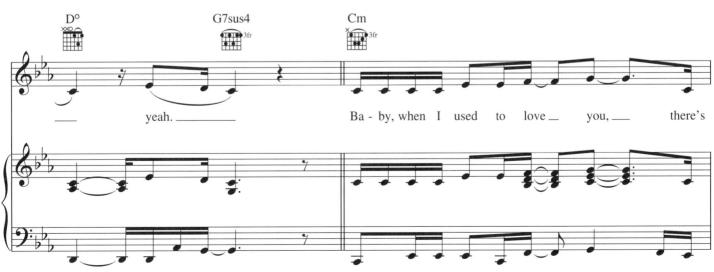

___ yeah. _____   Ba - by, when I used to love __ you, ___ there's

Alright

Words and Music by
John Stephens and Kanye West

Moderately slow

Yeah, ___ yeah, ___ yeah, ___ yeah, __ yeah, yeah, ___ yeah, __ yeah, __ yeah, __ yeah,

yeah, ___ yeah, __ yeah, __ yeah, __ yeah, yeah, ___ yeah, __ yeah, __ yeah, __ yeah.

O - K, ___ I see you check - in' me out. ___ I think I know what you're wink - in' a - bout. __
Good Lord, __ you got bod - y for days. __ I think the way that you shake it's a - maz - in'.

23

She Don't Have to Know

Words and Music by
John Stephens, Will Adams
and Sylvester Stewart

Though it's wrong, it's hard to tell the truth. Oh, no. _____ She don't have to

know. She don't have to know. When I meet _ ya, I

got my shades _ on to cov-er up my eyes,
(Just to cov-er _ up my eyes.)
hop-in' that no-bod-y sees me pass-in'

by through _ my dis-guise. _____ I still _ know _____ you'll rec -
(I still know.)

Number One

Words and Music by
John Stephens, Kanye West
and Curtis Mayfield

you can't see all I do to keep you from know-in' the things___ I do, like e-

rase my phone___ and keep it out-ta town. I keep it strapped up when I___ sleep a-round. Well,

I should-a known one day___ you'd find out, but you can't go and leave___ me now. You know that I love___

___ you. There's no one a-bove___ you.___ I said it the last___

To Codas I & II

time, _____ but this is the last ___ time. So don't make me o-

ver _____ 'cause I can be faith - ful. _____ You, ba - by, you're my

num - ber one. ___ You're my num - ber one. _ Now, "Who is she? What's her name?"

You don't need to know a - bout ev - 'ry - thing. _ We fight a - bout this, we fight a - bout that. You

Left with a hang - o - ver. I prom-ise I won't __ cheat. I prom-ise I won't __ lie. I
(You say we o - ver.)

prom-ise to act __ right. (You say we o - ver.) If you can't tell me I can't have you.

I can't have that. __ Hey, __ it ain't __
(We ain't o - ver.) __

40

I Can Change

Words and Music by
John Stephens, Calvin Broadus
and Dave Tozer

When to change. Like Sam Cooke say, change is gon' come, nephew. And you better believe that.

As I look back _ on all _ that I've done to you _____ (yeah), _____ my
I'll give up all _ the plac - es I used to go. _____ I'll

big - gest re - gret, _ the things that I nev - er could do _____ (yeah). _____
stay out the club _ and stay home be - cause _ I'm wit you, _____ yeah. _____

I see the light _ now, ba - by; it's shin - in' through. _ I got - ta
I'll give up all _ those girls that I used to know. _ But

*Substitute small notes 2nd time.

44

han-dle my bid-ness a-just like a real _ man should do. _____ (Yeah, _ hey, yeah, _ hey.)
eyes and I'm gon-na be much bet-ter for you, _____ yeah, _ hey. _____

I can change, I can change, **(You know I can change, _ ba -

*(Spoken:) Yeah. I'm willing to make that change, baby. I'm willing to make that change.

*3rd time only (spoken under vocals) **1st time only (2nd time ad lib)

I can change for _____ you. _____
by. You know I can stop, ba - by.

I mean, out of all the people in the world, who would've thought that the big boss Dogg would be willing to

I can change, I can change, Ooh, _____ yeah.) _
You know I can change, _ ba - by.

make that change. Yeah, you're special, baby. You're real special. You're gettin' the pimp to leave all his

Ordinary People

Words and Music by
John Stephens and Will Adams

we should take __ it slow. __ We're __ just or - di-nar-y peo - ple. __

We __ don't know __ which __ way to go, __ 'cause __ we're or - di-nar-y peo -

ple. __ May - be we __ should take it slow. __ Take it

slow, oh, __ oh. __ This time we'll take __ it slow. __

Stay with You

Words and Music by
John Stephens and Dave Tozer

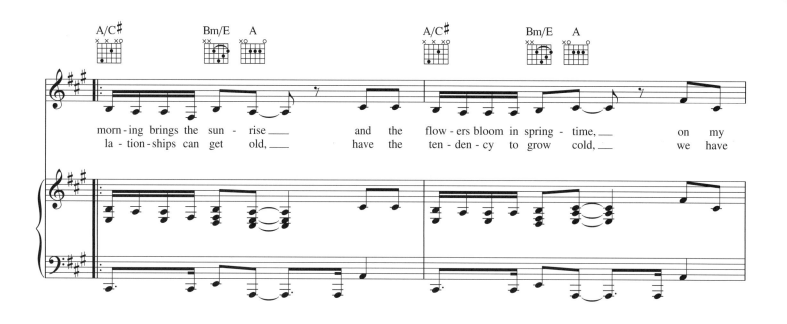

morn - ing brings the sun - rise ___ and the flow - ers bloom in spring - time, ___ on my
la - tion - ships can get old, ___ have the ten - den - cy to grow cold, ___ we have

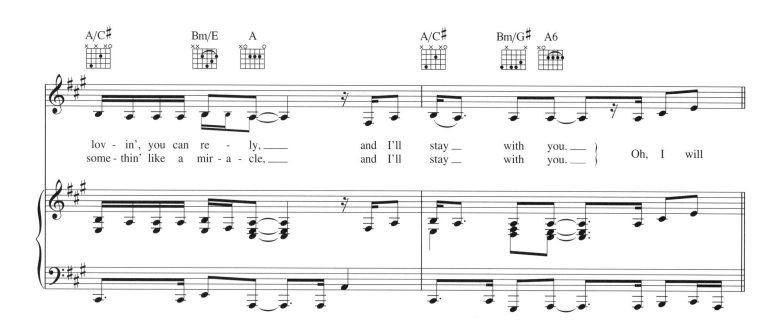

lov - in', you can re - ly, ___ and I'll stay ___ with you. ___ } Oh, I will
some - thin' like a mir - a - cle, ___ and I'll stay ___ with you. ___ }

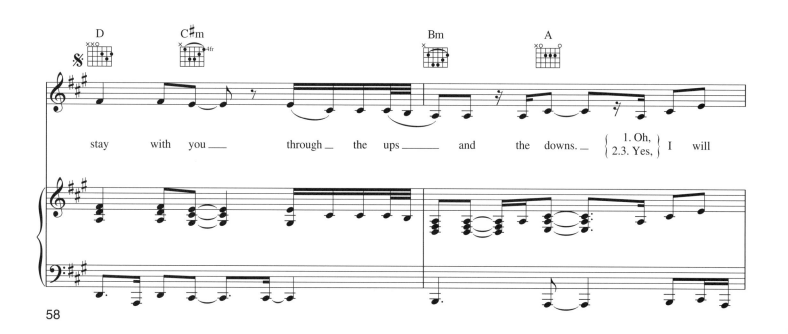

stay with you ___ through ___ the ups ___ and the downs. ___ { 1. Oh, } I will
{ 2.3. Yes, }

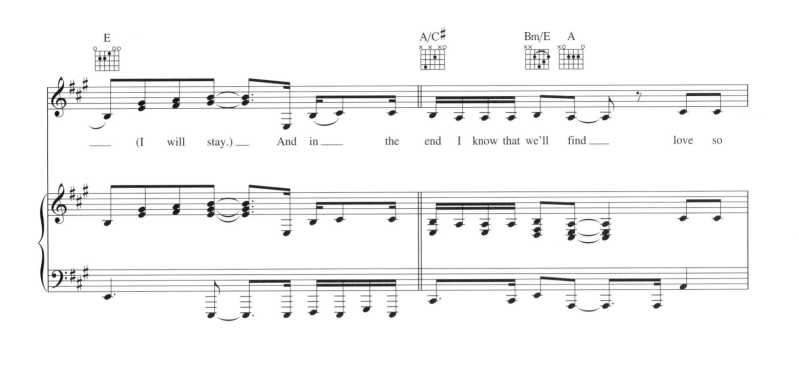

(I will stay.) And in the end I know that we'll find love so

beau-ti-ful and di-vine. And we'll be lov-ers for a life-time, yeah, and I'll

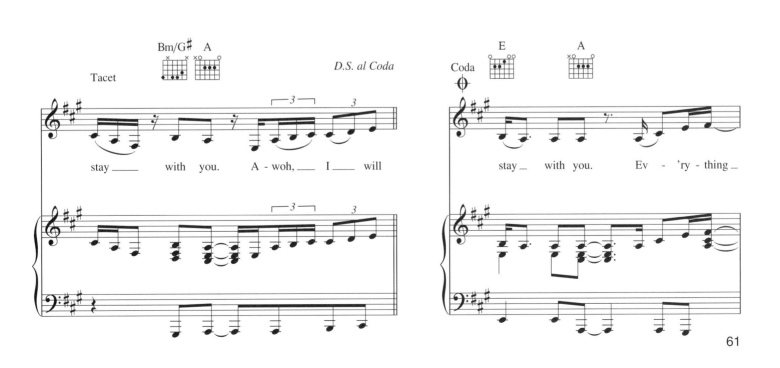

stay with you. A-woh, I will stay with you. Ev-'ry-thing

D.S. al Coda

Coda

will be fine, yeah, and I'll stay with you. Through the

end of all time, I will stay with you. Ooh,

ooh.

Let's Get Lifted Again

Words and Music by
John Stephens and Dave Tozer

Moderately slow

Come and go with me. There's so much new to see. Get

high with me. Come fly with me. Ooh, I want you so. I'm a-

bout to lose con-trol. ___ Get high ___ with me. Come fly with me.

Vocal ad lib...

So ___ much, ___

so much, _ I wan-na show you. ___ Ah, ___ so ___ much,

So High

Words and Music by
John Stephens, DeVon Harris, Paul Cho,
Leon Ware and Pamela Sawyer

Moderately

with pedal

Ba - by, since the day you came __ in - to __ my life, __

May - be lat - er we can go __ up to __ the moon __

you made me re - al - ize __ that we were born __ to fly. __

or sail a - mong the stars __ be - fore __ the night __ is through. __

ooh, this feels so cra - zy. Oh, this love is blaz - in'.

And ba - by, we're so high, walk - in' on cloud

nine. So high, so

high. Woh.

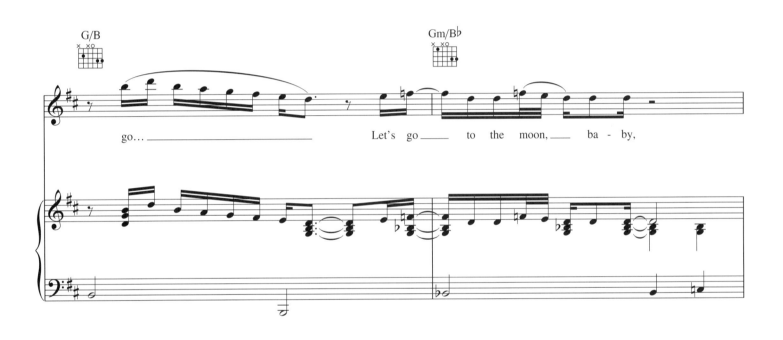

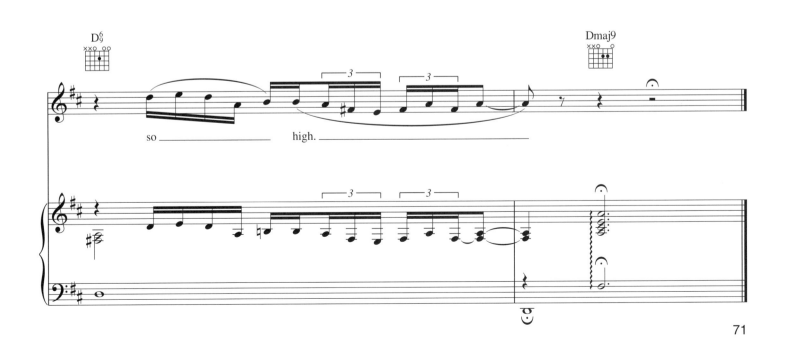

Refuge

(When It's Cold Outside)

Words and Music by
John Stephens, DeVon Harris
and Paul Cho

Moderately

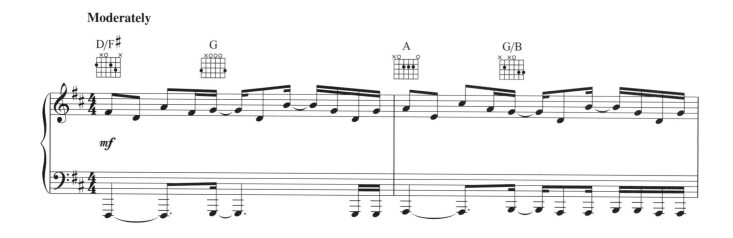

I prayed for bet - ter days   to come.   I prayed that I   would see   the sun. ___
Now, peace is   so hard   to find.   We're ter - ror-ized   and vic - tim - ized. ___

'Cause life is so bur - den - some when ev - 'ry day's a rain - y one.
But that's when I close my eyes and think of you to ease my mind.

But sud - den - ly there's _ no more clouds. And I be - lieve with - out a doubt _
You take me to an - oth - er place where there's no more war, just love and grace. _

that heav - en sent an an - gel down _ and then she turned my _ life a - round.
And ba - by, you re - store my faith. _ I know this strug - gle's _ not in vain.

And you know and I _ know _ friends come and friends _ go. _
And you know and I _ know, _ through all the bat - tles, _

73

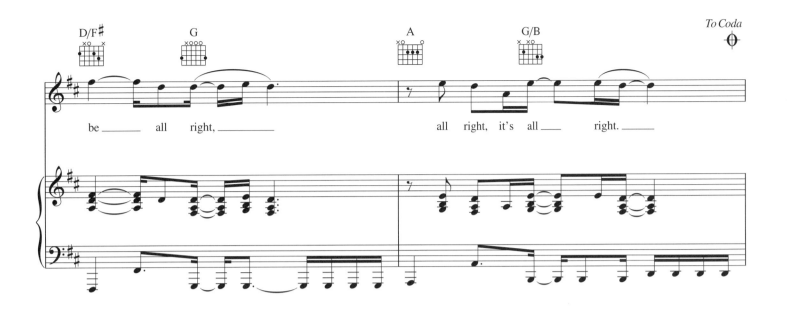

be ___ all right, ___ all right, it's all ___ right. ___

1.

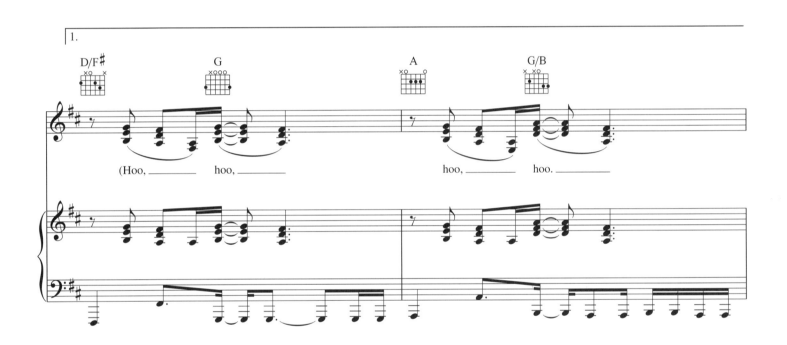

(Hoo, ___ hoo, ___ hoo, ___ hoo. ___

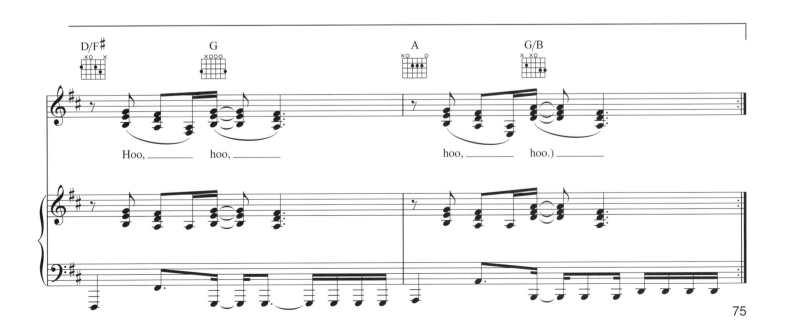

Hoo, ___ hoo, ___ hoo, ___ hoo.) ___

It Don't Have to Change

Words and Music by
John Stephens and Dave Tozer

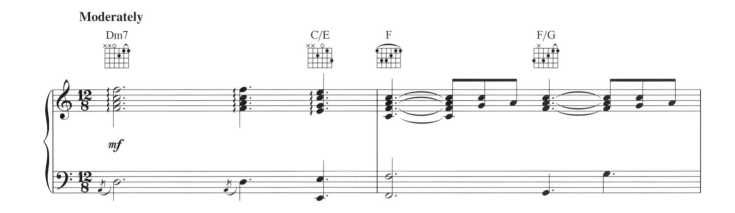

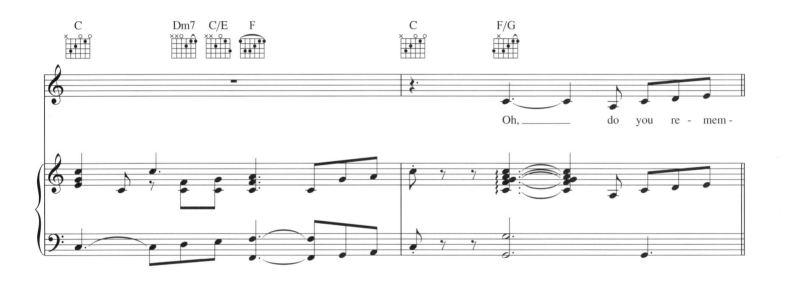

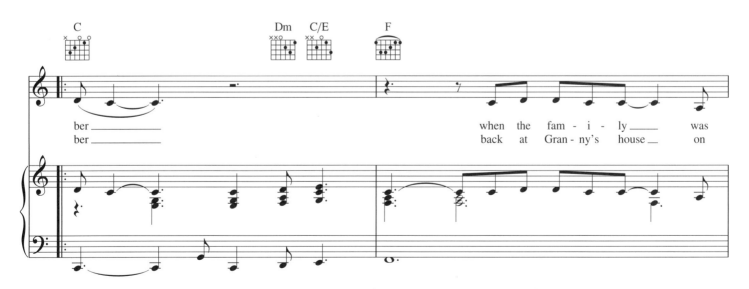

Live It Up

Words and Music by
John Stephens, Anthony Hester,
DeVon Harris and Tarey Torae

know, ___ we've been strug - gl - ing for such a long ___ time, work - ing here and there just to get ___
more ___ put - tin' it in the lay - a - way, 'cause, boo, I got the mon - ey to -

by. ___ It's fi - n'lly time for me to get ___ mine. No
day. ___ Come on and go to the mall and let's ___ play. Let's

more ___ rob - bin' Pe - ter so we could pay ___ Paul or go'n' to ma - ma's house to make a phone ___
go ___ raise a toast to the days a - head. You can't take it with you when you're ___

call. ___ No, we don't have to strug - gle at ___ all. 'Cause _____ now ___
dead. ___ You might as well en - joy it now in - stead. Oh, _____ now ___

ev-'ry day is feel-ing like Fri-day. ____ I'm get-tin' paid and do-in' it my way. ____
it's a-bout to be a long eve-nin'. ____ We'll par-ty through the rest of the week-end. ____

We're fi-n'lly on our way. Ba-by, now it's ____ time to cel-e-brate. ____ Oh, ____

live it up; we can go cra-zy. Live it up; you and me, ba-by.

Live it up, live it up, live it up. We're

fly - in' high; ___ don't wan-na come down. We'll let 'em know all o - ver town and

live it up, ___ live it up, live it up. No

live it up. (We can fly so high in the moon - lit sky, cuz there's

no more cloud - y days. It's so beau - ti - ful ___ when you feel the flow. ___ We can

Do you re-mem-ber when times were hard, _____ oh, so hard?
dance the night a-way.)   (Oh, so hard.

Through it all, _____ we've come so far. _____   So we got-ta
We've come so far.   Hah, hah,   hah, hah.)

live it up. _____   So we can just cel-e-brate. _____ There's no more pain.
                                                                 (There's no more pain.

Raise your glass _____ and feel no shame. _____   Oh, _____   so we got-ta
And feel no shame. _____   Hah, hah,   hah, hah.)

live it up. _____ Ah, _____ oh, _____

Coda

live it up.

Vocal ad lib...

Play 4 times

Mm. _

It's time to cel - e - brate, ba - by.

L.H.

Hey, we got - ta live it up. _____

(Hah, hah, hah, hah, ooh.)

rit. **pp**